Coping with Bipolar

Practical Tools for Daily Living.

Copyright Notice

Disclaimer

This book falls within the realm of nonfiction in the field of health. The information presented here is intended solely for general informational purposes and should not be considered a replacement for professional medical advice, diagnosis, or treatment. It is imperative to always seek guidance from a qualified healthcare provider or physician regarding any inquiries you may have about a medical condition. Please do not disregard professional medical advice or delay seeking it based on the content found in this book.

Contents

Introduction

In the labyrinth of the human mind, where emotions weave an intricate tapestry, there exists a dynamic interplay that challenges the very essence of our existence. For those navigating the turbulent waters of bipolar disorder, this intricate dance can become a formidable journey—one marked by the highs of euphoria and the lows of despair. "Coping with Bipolar: Practical Tools for Daily Living" is a compass for those seeking to navigate this intricate terrain with resilience, offering a guide through the peaks and valleys of bipolar disorder.

In these pages, we embark on a voyage of understanding, compassion, and empowerment. The canvas we paint is one of practical tools designed to illuminate the path toward stability, resilience, and a meaningful daily life. From the depths of despair to the heights of self-discovery, each chapter unfolds as a stepping stone toward a more balanced and fulfilling life.

As we delve into the practical tools within these pages, may they serve as beacons of hope, lighting the way for individuals, their loved ones, and the community that surrounds them. Together, let us embark on a journey of understanding, acceptance, and resilience—a journey toward not merely surviving but thriving in the face of bipolar disorder.

Chapter 2

Bipolar Disorder

Bipolar disorder, formerly known as manic-depressive illness, is a complex mental health condition that affects millions of people worldwide. Characterized by extreme mood swings, individuals with bipolar disorder experience episodes of intense mania or hypomania, alternating with periods of deep depression. In this chapter, we will delve into the various types and symptoms of bipolar disorder, as well as explore the potential causes and triggers that contribute to its onset.

Types and Symptoms of Bipolar Disorder

Types of Bipolar Disorder

1. **Bipolar I Disorder:** Characterized by manic episodes that last at least seven days or by manic symptoms that are so severe that immediate hospitalization is required. Depressive episodes typically last for at least two weeks.

2. **Bipolar II Disorder:** Involves a pattern of depressive episodes and hypomanic episodes (less severe than full-blown mania) but no full-blown manic or mixed episodes.

3. **Cyclothymic Disorder:** This is a milder form of bipolar disorder characterized by periods of hypomanic symptoms as well

as periods of depressive symptoms. The symptoms are less severe than those of bipolar I or II.

Symptoms of Mania (in Bipolar I and II)

1. **Elevated or Irritable Mood:** Feeling unusually happy, optimistic, or agitated.

2. **Increased Energy and Activity:** Engaging in activities with a higher level of intensity, often without considering the consequences.

3. **Decreased Need for Sleep:** Feeling rested after very little sleep.

4. **Rapid Speech and Racing Thoughts:** Speaking quickly and having an abundance of thoughts that may be difficult to follow.

5. **Poor Judgment:** Engaging in risky behaviors without considering the potential negative outcomes.

Symptoms of Depression

1. **Persistent Sadness or Anxiety:** Feeling sad, empty, or anxious for an extended period.

2. **Lack of Interest in Activities:** Losing interest in activities once enjoyed.

3. **Fatigue and Decreased Energy:** Feeling tired and having low energy levels.

4. **Sleep Disturbances:** Changes in sleep patterns, such as insomnia or oversleeping.

5. **Difficulty Concentrating:** Problems with memory and concentration.

6. **Feelings of Guilt or Worthlessness:**
Experiencing feelings of guilt or a
diminished sense of self-worth.

Causes and Triggers of Bipolar Disorder

The exact causes of bipolar disorder are not fully understood, and it likely involves a combination of genetic, neurobiological, and environmental factors. Researchers continue to investigate these factors to gain a better understanding of the disorder. Here are some key considerations regarding the potential causes and triggers of bipolar disorder:

Genetic Factors

1. **Family History:** Bipolar disorder tends to run in families, suggesting a genetic component. Individuals with a first-degree relative (parent or sibling) with bipolar disorder have a higher risk of developing the condition.

2. **Genetic Markers:** Some studies have identified specific genetic markers associated with an increased susceptibility to bipolar disorder. However, genetic factors alone are not sufficient to cause the disorder.

Neurobiological Factors

1. **Neurotransmitter Imbalances:** Imbalances in neurotransmitters, such as serotonin, dopamine, and

norepinephrine, are thought to play a role in bipolar disorder. These neurotransmitters are involved in regulating mood, and disruptions in their function may contribute to mood swings.

2. **Brain Structure and Function:** Structural and functional abnormalities in certain brain regions, including the prefrontal cortex and amygdala, have been observed in individuals with bipolar disorder. These abnormalities may impact emotional regulation and mood stability.

Environmental Factors

1. **Stressful Life Events:** High levels of stress, trauma, or major life changes can act as triggers for the onset of bipolar episodes. Stressful events may not

directly cause bipolar disorder but can contribute to the manifestation of symptoms in genetically predisposed individuals.

2. **Substance Abuse:** Substance abuse, including alcohol and drug misuse, can exacerbate or trigger episodes of bipolar disorder. It's important to note that substance abuse does not cause bipolar disorder but can significantly impact its course.

3. **Sleep Disturbances:** Disruptions in sleep patterns, such as insomnia or irregular sleep schedules, can be both a cause and a trigger for bipolar episodes. Sleep disturbances are known to influence mood stability.

4. **Seasonal Changes:** Some individuals with bipolar disorder may experience a seasonal pattern to their mood episodes, with manic or depressive episodes more likely to occur during specific times of the year.

Hormonal Factors

1. **Hormonal Changes:** Hormonal fluctuations, such as those associated with the menstrual cycle or pregnancy, may influence the onset or exacerbation of bipolar symptoms in some individuals.

Medication-Induced

1. **Certain Medications:** In some cases, the use of certain medications, such as antidepressants or corticosteroids, can trigger manic episodes in individuals with

bipolar disorder.

Bipolar disorder is a multifaceted mental health condition with various types and a spectrum of symptoms. While genetic factors and neurochemical imbalances contribute significantly, environmental triggers and disruptions in biological rhythms also play a crucial role. Understanding the complexities of bipolar disorder is essential for effective diagnosis, treatment, and ongoing management. As research progresses, it is hoped that advancements in our understanding of the disorder will lead to more targeted and personalized approaches to care, improving the quality of life for those affected by bipolar disorder.

Chapter 2

The Rollercoaster Ride

Living with bipolar disorder often feels like riding an emotional rollercoaster, with highs of mania and lows of depression. Navigating these mood swings can be challenging, but understanding and recognizing the different phases is crucial for effective management. Let's now explore the distinctive features of mania and depression, offering insights into recognizing and understanding each state and providing strategies for managing and coping with the intense fluctuations.

Recognizing and Understanding Mania

1. **Elevated Mood and Energy:** Mania is characterized by an intense and persistent elevation in mood. Individuals may feel excessively happy, euphoric, or irritable. Energy levels soar, often leading to increased activity, restlessness, and a reduced need for sleep.

2. **Racing Thoughts and Impulsivity:** Thoughts during manic episodes can race, making it challenging to concentrate or stay focused. Impulsivity and poor decision-making are common, leading to actions that may have long-term consequences.

3. **Grandiosity:** Individuals experiencing

mania may develop an inflated sense of self-importance or grandiosity. This can manifest as unrealistic beliefs about one's abilities, leading to risky behaviors.

4. **Increased Sociability:** Manic episodes are often associated with heightened sociability, increased talkativeness, and a desire for constant social interaction.

Managing and Coping with Depression

Recognizing Depressive Symptoms

Depression in bipolar disorder is characterized by persistent feelings of sadness, hopelessness, and a lack of interest in activities.

Changes in sleep patterns, appetite, and

energy levels are common, and individuals may experience fatigue and difficulty concentrating. Here are some strategies for managing and coping with depression in bipolar disorder:

1. **Medication Management:**

- Mood stabilizers and atypical antipsychotics are commonly prescribed to manage bipolar disorder. These medications help regulate mood and reduce the severity and frequency of depressive episodes.

- It's essential to take prescribed medications consistently and communicate openly with healthcare providers about any side effects or concerns.

2.   **Therapy:**

- Psychotherapy, such as cognitive-behavioral therapy (CBT) or interpersonal therapy, can be beneficial. These approaches can help individuals identify and challenge negative thought patterns, develop coping strategies, and improve interpersonal relationships.

3.   **Education and Self-awareness:**

- Understanding the nature of bipolar disorder, including its cycles and triggers, can empower individuals to better manage their condition. Self-awareness helps in recognizing early signs of depressive episodes, allowing for prompt intervention.

4. **Lifestyle Changes:**

- Maintaining a regular sleep schedule is crucial, as disruptions in sleep patterns can trigger mood episodes. Establishing a routine that includes sufficient sleep is essential for mood stability.

- Regular exercise has been shown to have positive effects on mood. Even moderate physical activity can help alleviate symptoms of depression.

5. **Social Support:**

- Building a strong support system is vital. Friends, family, and support groups can offer understanding, encouragement, and assistance during challenging times.

- Educating close friends and family about bipolar disorder can help them provide effective support and recognize signs of depressive episodes.

6. **Mindfulness and Stress Reduction:**

- Mindfulness techniques, such as meditation and deep breathing exercises, can be valuable in managing stress and promoting emotional well-being.

- Identifying and managing stressors is crucial, as stress can contribute to mood fluctuations in individuals with bipolar disorder.

7. **Regular Monitoring and Check-ins:**

- Regular check-ins with mental health professionals can help monitor mood stability and adjust treatment plans as needed.

- Keeping a mood journal to track daily moods, sleep patterns, and potential triggers can provide valuable information for both individuals and their healthcare providers.

8.   **Crisis Planning:**

- Developing a crisis plan that includes strategies for managing severe depressive episodes, such as contacting healthcare providers or seeking emergency assistance, is important for overall safety.

Navigating the rollercoaster ride of bipolar disorder involves recognizing the distinctive features of mania and depression and implementing effective strategies for management. Whether through medication adherence, therapeutic interventions, or lifestyle modifications, individuals with bipolar disorder can gain a sense of control over their mood swings. Building a strong support system is paramount, ensuring that the journey through the highs and lows is not undertaken alone. With the right tools and support, individuals with bipolar disorder can lead fulfilling lives, managing the twists and turns of their emotional rollercoaster.

Chapter 3

Building a Support System

In the complex landscape of mental health, the importance of a robust support system cannot be overstated. For individuals facing challenges such as bipolar disorder, depression, anxiety, or any other mental health condition, a support network plays a crucial role in providing understanding, encouragement, and assistance. This chapter explores the pivotal roles that family and friends, as well as professional help, play in building a comprehensive and effective support system.

The Role of Family and Friends

1. **Understanding and Empathy:** Family and friends serve as the first line of defense in understanding and empathizing with the challenges faced by someone dealing with mental health issues. Educating loved ones about the condition fosters empathy and reduces stigma, creating an environment where open communication can thrive.

2. **Active Listening:** A supportive network involves active listening – the ability to hear and understand without judgment. This creates a safe space for individuals to express their thoughts and feelings. Encouraging open dialogue helps in sharing experiences and enables loved

ones to provide emotional support effectively.

3. **Assistance in Daily Life:** Practical support is vital, especially during challenging periods. This may involve helping with daily tasks, providing meals, or assisting in creating a structured routine. Offering tangible assistance not only eases the burden on the individual but also reinforces a sense of care and solidarity.

4. **Participating in Treatment Plans:** Involving family and friends in treatment plans fosters a collaborative approach to mental health care. Attending therapy sessions or psychiatrist appointments together can enhance mutual understanding and contribute to more

effective support.

Seeking Professional Help

Seeking professional help is a crucial and positive step for individuals with bipolar disorder because managing this condition can be challenging. Therefore, professional assistance is often essential for effective treatment and support. Here are some key points to consider:

1. **Accurate Diagnosis:** Bipolar disorder can be challenging to diagnose, as its symptoms may overlap with other mental health conditions. Consulting with a mental health professional, such as a psychiatrist or psychologist, can help ensure an accurate diagnosis. This is

essential for developing an appropriate treatment plan.

2. **Medication Management:** Medications are commonly prescribed to stabilize mood swings and manage symptoms. A psychiatrist is usually the primary healthcare provider for prescribing and monitoring medication. It's important for individuals with bipolar disorder to work closely with their healthcare team to find the most effective medication and dosage for their specific needs.

3. **Therapeutic Support:** Psychotherapy, such as cognitive-behavioral therapy (CBT) or dialectical behavior therapy (DBT), can be beneficial in managing bipolar disorder. These therapies can help

individuals understand and cope with the impact of their condition, develop effective coping strategies, and improve interpersonal relationships.

4. **Regular Monitoring and Adjustments:** Bipolar disorder often requires ongoing monitoring and adjustments to treatment plans. Regular check-ins with a mental health professional allow for the evaluation of treatment effectiveness, the identification of potential triggers, and the adjustment of medications or therapeutic approaches as needed.

5. **Education and Self-Management:** Professionals can provide valuable education about bipolar disorder, helping individuals understand their condition

and recognize early warning signs of mood episodes. This knowledge empowers individuals to actively participate in their treatment and practice self-management strategies.

6. **Crisis Intervention:** In times of crisis, having a mental health professional to turn to is crucial. They can provide immediate support, help navigate emergency services, and work with individuals to develop crisis plans for managing severe mood episodes.

Building a support system is a collaborative effort that involves the active participation of both loved ones and mental health professionals. The synergy between family, friends, and professionals creates a holistic framework that addresses the diverse needs of individuals facing mental health challenges. By fostering understanding, empathy, and practical assistance, a strong support system becomes a cornerstone for emotional resilience, providing a foundation for individuals to navigate the complexities of their mental health journey with strength and optimism.

Chapter 4

Medication Management

Medication management is a pivotal aspect of treating bipolar disorder. The delicate balance of pharmacological interventions aims to stabilize mood, prevent relapses, and enhance the overall quality of life for individuals with bipolar disorder. In this chapter, we'll explore the diverse landscape of bipolar medications, emphasizing the importance of adherence and effective side effect management in achieving treatment success.

Overview of Bipolar Medications

Here's an overview of the main classes of medications used to treat bipolar disorder:

1. **Mood Stabilizers:**

- *Lithium:* Lithium has been a mainstay in the treatment of bipolar disorder for decades. It is effective in reducing the frequency and severity of manic episodes. Regular blood tests are necessary to monitor lithium levels and ensure its safety and efficacy.

- *Valproic Acid (Depakote):* Valproic acid is another mood stabilizer that is often used to treat bipolar disorder. It is effective in managing manic episodes and is sometimes used in combination with other medications.

2. **Antipsychotics:**

- *Atypical Antipsychotics:* Medications such as quetiapine (Seroquel), olanzapine (Zyprexa), risperidone (Risperdal), and aripiprazole (Abilify) are often prescribed to help manage both manic and depressive episodes. These medications can also be used as maintenance therapy to prevent relapses.

3. **Antidepressants:**

- *Selective Serotonin Reuptake Inhibitors (SSRIs):* While SSRIs are commonly used to treat depression, they are used cautiously in bipolar disorder, often in combination with mood stabilizers or antipsychotics. The use of antidepressants alone in bipolar disorder can potentially trigger manic episodes.

- *Serotonin-Norepinephrine Reuptake Inhibitors (SNRIs):* Similar to SSRIs, SNRIs like venlafaxine (Effexor) may be used cautiously in combination with mood stabilizers.

4. **Anticonvulsants:**

- In addition to valproic acid, other anticonvulsant medications such as carbamazepine (Tegretol) and lamotrigine (Lamictal) may be prescribed. Lamotrigine, in particular, is often used for long-term maintenance treatment to prevent depressive episodes.

5.   **Benzodiazepines:**

- Benzodiazepines, such as lorazepam or clonazepam, may be prescribed for short-term relief of acute symptoms, especially during manic episodes or periods of severe anxiety.

6.   **Electroconvulsive Therapy (ECT):**

- In some cases where medications are not effective or are not well-tolerated, electroconvulsive therapy may be considered. ECT is a medical treatment that involves passing a small, carefully controlled amount of electrical current through the brain to induce a therapeutic seizure.

Significance of Following Bipolar Disorder Treatment

Adherence to medication is crucial in the effective management of bipolar disorder. Medications play a pivotal role in stabilizing mood, preventing relapses, and improving overall functioning. Here are several reasons why adherence to bipolar medication is so important:

1. **Stabilizing Mood Swings:** Bipolar medications, such as mood stabilizers, antipsychotics, and sometimes antidepressants, work to regulate mood and minimize the intensity and frequency of mood swings. Adherence to the prescribed medication regimen helps maintain a stable mood, reducing the

likelihood of manic or depressive episodes.

2. **Preventing Relapses:** Bipolar disorder is often characterized by periods of remission and relapse. Adhering to the prescribed medication plan is associated with a reduced risk of relapse. Consistent medication use helps maintain the therapeutic effects, preventing the recurrence of mood episodes and minimizing the impact on daily life.

3. **Improving Functioning:** Medication adherence is linked to better overall functioning in individuals with bipolar disorder. Stable moods enable individuals to manage their responsibilities, maintain relationships, and pursue personal and

professional goals. Improved functioning contributes to a better quality of life.

4. **Reducing Hospitalizations and Emergency Care:** Non-adherence to medication is a common reason for hospitalizations and emergency room visits among individuals with bipolar disorder. Adhering to medication helps prevent severe mood episodes that may require acute interventions, reducing the need for hospitalizations and emergency care.

5. **Enhancing Treatment Efficacy:** Bipolar medications are most effective when taken consistently as prescribed. Adherence ensures that the therapeutic levels of the medication are maintained in

the body, optimizing their effectiveness in managing symptoms and preventing the recurrence of mood episodes.

6. **Minimizing Disruption to Daily Life:** Inconsistent medication use can lead to disruptions in daily life due to the unpredictable nature of mood swings. Adherence helps individuals maintain a more predictable and manageable lifestyle, reducing the impact of bipolar symptoms on relationships, work, and other aspects of daily living.

7. **Fostering Long-Term Stability:** Bipolar disorder is a chronic condition that requires ongoing management. Adherence to medication contributes to long-term stability, allowing individuals to

sustain improvements in mood and overall well-being over extended periods.

Medication Side Effects

Bipolar medications, including mood stabilizers, antipsychotics, and antidepressants, can be effective in managing symptoms, but like any medications, they can also have side effects. It's important to note that the specific side effects can vary depending on the type of medication and the individual's response. Here are some common side effects associated with medications used to treat bipolar disorder:

1. **Mood Stabilizers:**

- **Lithium:** A widely used mood stabilizer.

Side effects may include hand tremors, increased thirst and urination, weight gain, and thyroid or kidney function changes.

- **Anticonvulsants (e.g., valproic acid, lamotrigine):** These medications may cause dizziness, drowsiness, gastrointestinal issues, and in some cases, an increased risk of liver problems.

2. **Antipsychotics:**

- **Olanzapine, quetiapine, risperidone, aripiprazole, etc.:** Common side effects include weight gain, sedation, increased cholesterol levels, and the potential for metabolic issues like diabetes.

- **Extrapyramidal symptoms (EPS):** These can include tremors, stiffness, and involuntary movements and are more common with typical antipsychotics.

3. **Antidepressants:**

- **Selective serotonin reuptake inhibitors (SSRIs) or serotonin-norepinephrine reuptake inhibitors (SNRIs):** While these are sometimes prescribed for depressive episodes, they may induce manic episodes in individuals with bipolar disorder. Additionally, they can cause insomnia, sexual dysfunction, and weight changes.

4. **Benzodiazepines:**

- **Used for anxiety or insomnia:** Can cause drowsiness, dizziness, and dependency with long-term use. Abrupt discontinuation can lead to withdrawal symptoms.

5. **Common Side Effects Across Medications:**

- **Weight Gain:** Many bipolar medications are associated with weight gain, which can contribute to other health issues.

- **Sedation:** Some medications can cause drowsiness or fatigue, particularly at the beginning of treatment.

- **Cognitive Impairment:** Some individuals may experience difficulties with concentration and memory.

- **Gastrointestinal Issues:** Nausea, upset stomach, or diarrhea may occur with certain medications.

Side Effect management

Managing side effects of bipolar medication is an essential aspect of ensuring treatment adherence and overall well-being for individuals with bipolar disorder. Here's a discussion about managing the side effect of bipolar medications:

1. **Adherence Improvement:** Addressing side effects promptly can enhance medication adherence. If individuals experience unpleasant side effects, they may be less likely to continue taking their medications as prescribed. Effective side effect management promotes a more positive experience with medication, increasing the likelihood that individuals will adhere to their treatment plan.

2. **Communication with Healthcare Providers:** Open communication between individuals and their healthcare providers is crucial. Patients should report any side effects promptly, enabling healthcare professionals to adjust treatment plans as needed. Regular check-ins can help monitor side effects and ensure that the chosen medications are both effective and tolerable.

3. **Individualized Treatment Plans:** Bipolar disorder is a heterogeneous condition, and individuals may react differently to medications. Tailoring treatment plans to the specific needs and tolerances of each patient is essential. Adjustments in dosage, switching

medications, or using adjunctive medications to manage side effects can be part of an individualized approach.

4. **Education and Expectation Management:** Providing education about potential side effects before starting medication can help manage expectations. Knowing what to anticipate and understanding that not all side effects are permanent or intolerable can empower individuals to navigate the initial phases of medication use more effectively.

5. **Regular Monitoring:** Regular monitoring of both therapeutic effects and side effects is essential. Healthcare providers may conduct regular check-ups,

blood tests, or other assessments to ensure that the medication is working as intended and that any emerging side effects are addressed promptly.

6.   **Lifestyle Modifications:** In some cases, lifestyle modifications can help manage side effects. For instance, changes in diet, exercise, or sleep patterns might alleviate certain side effects or improve overall well-being. Healthcare providers may offer guidance on such adjustments.

7.   **Psychosocial Support:** Addressing the psychosocial impact of side effects is crucial. Some side effects may affect an individual's self-esteem, body image, or overall quality of life. Providing psychosocial support, such as counseling

or support groups, can help individuals cope with these challenges.

Medication management in bipolar disorder is indeed a balancing act, requiring collaboration between individuals, healthcare providers, and often, a multidisciplinary team. The diverse array of medications available offers flexibility in tailoring treatment plans to individual needs. Adherence and effective side effect management are the cornerstones of successful treatment, allowing individuals to navigate the complex terrain of bipolar disorder with greater stability and improved overall quality of life. As research continues to advance, the hope is that more targeted and personalized pharmacological interventions will emerge, further refining the delicate balance required in managing bipolar disorder.

Chapter 5

Daily Routines for Stability

In the realm of mental health, the importance of daily routines cannot be overstated. For individuals managing conditions like bipolar disorder, establishing and maintaining stable daily routines is a key component of a holistic approach to well-being. In this chapter, we'll explore the critical role of consistent sleep patterns, as well as the impact of nutrition and exercise in promoting stability and resilience in daily life.

Effect of Establishing Consistent Sleep Patterns

Establishing consistent sleep patterns can play a crucial role in managing bipolar disorder. The impact of sleep on bipolar patients is significant, as disruptions in sleep can trigger episodes and exacerbate symptoms.

1. **Stabilizing Mood Swings:**

- **Manic Episodes:** Lack of sleep or irregular sleep patterns can contribute to the onset of manic episodes. However, consistent sleep helps stabilize mood and reduce the likelihood of excessive energy, impulsivity, and heightened irritability associated with mania.

- **Depressive Episodes:** On the other hand, establishing a regular sleep routine can help mitigate depressive symptoms. Sleep consistency aids in maintaining a more stable emotional state, reducing the severity and duration of depressive episodes.

2. **Regulating Circadian Rhythms:** Bipolar disorder often involves disruptions in circadian rhythms, the body's natural internal clock. Consistent sleep patterns help regulate these rhythms, promoting a sense of balance in hormonal and neurotransmitter release, which can positively impact mood regulation.

3. **Enhancing Medication Efficacy:** Many bipolar patients are prescribed

medications to stabilize their moods. Consistent sleep patterns can enhance the effectiveness of these medications. Medication adherence combined with a regular sleep routine contributes to better overall symptom management.

4. **Preventing Triggers and Relapses:** Sleep disruptions act as triggers for both manic and depressive episodes. By maintaining a consistent sleep schedule, individuals with bipolar disorder can reduce the risk of relapses and better manage stressors that may contribute to the recurrence of symptoms.

5. **Improving Cognitive Function:** Bipolar disorder can impact cognitive function, including concentration and memory.

Quality sleep is essential for cognitive health. Consistent sleep patterns support improved cognitive function, aiding individuals in coping with the cognitive challenges associated with bipolar disorder.

How to Establish a Consistent Sleep Pattern

Establishing consistent sleep patterns for individuals with bipolar disorder requires a combination of lifestyle adjustments, routine development, and ongoing self-awareness. Here are some practical strategies for bipolar patients to promote consistent sleep:

1. **Create a Sleep Schedule:** Set a consistent bedtime and wake-up time,

aiming for at least 7-9 hours of sleep per night. Even on weekends, try to stick to the same sleep schedule to regulate the body's internal clock.

2. **Prioritize Sleep Hygiene:** Develop a bedtime routine that signals the body it's time to wind down. This can include activities like reading, taking a warm bath, or practicing relaxation techniques. Avoid stimulating activities close to bedtime.

3. **Optimize the Sleep Environment:** Ensure the bedroom is conducive to sleep by keeping it cool, dark, and quiet. Invest in a comfortable mattress and pillows. Minimize noise and light disturbances that could disrupt sleep.

4.   **Limit Stimulants and Alcohol:** Avoid stimulants such as caffeine and nicotine in the hours leading up to bedtime. Additionally, limit alcohol intake, as it can interfere with the quality of sleep.

5.   **Exercise Regularly:** Engage in regular physical activity, but try to complete exercise sessions earlier in the day. Exercise can promote better sleep, but intense physical activity close to bedtime may have a stimulating effect.

6.   **Monitor Medications:** Work closely with healthcare providers to ensure that medications do not interfere with sleep. Some medications may have sedating effects, while others may contribute to insomnia. Discuss any concerns or side

effects with the prescribing healthcare professional.

7.   **Manage Stress:** Practice stress-reduction techniques such as mindfulness, deep breathing, or meditation. Managing stress is crucial for individuals with bipolar disorder, as stress can trigger episodes and disrupt sleep.

8.   **Limit Napping:** If daytime napping is necessary, keep it short (20-30 minutes) and schedule it earlier in the day to avoid interfering with nighttime sleep.

9.   **Track Sleep Patterns:** Use a sleep diary or a mobile app to track sleep patterns, including bedtime, wake-up time, and any factors that may affect sleep. This information can be valuable for

identifying trends and making adjustments.

10. **Seek Professional Guidance:** Regularly communicate with mental health professionals, including psychiatrists and therapists, about sleep patterns and any challenges faced. They can provide guidance, make necessary adjustments to the treatment plan, and offer additional support.

11. **Educate Yourself:** Learn about the relationship between bipolar disorder and sleep. Understanding how sleep impacts mood can empower individuals to prioritize healthy sleep habits as an integral part of managing their condition.

The Impact of Nutrition and Exercise

Nutrition and exercise play crucial roles in the overall well-being of individuals with bipolar disorder. While they are not substitutes for medical treatment, incorporating healthy eating habits and regular physical activity can provide several benefits for bipolar patients:

1. **Mood Stabilization:** Balanced nutrition and regular exercise contribute to mood stabilization. Nutrient-rich foods and physical activity have been linked to the production of neurotransmitters like serotonin and dopamine, which play key roles in regulating mood.

2. **Improved Energy Levels:** Proper nutrition and exercise can enhance

energy levels, addressing the fatigue often associated with bipolar disorder. Maintaining stable energy throughout the day can contribute to better functioning and an improved sense of well-being.

3.   **Better Sleep Quality:** Both nutrition and exercise can positively impact sleep patterns. Establishing a healthy diet and engaging in regular physical activity can help regulate circadian rhythms, promoting better sleep quality, which is crucial for individuals with bipolar disorder.

4.   **Stress Reduction:** Nutrient-dense foods and exercise are known to have stress-reducing effects. Managing stress is particularly important for individuals

with bipolar disorder, as stress can trigger episodes. A balanced diet and regular physical activity can be valuable tools in stress management.

5. **Weight Management:** Some medications used to treat bipolar disorder may contribute to weight gain. Engaging in regular exercise and maintaining a balanced diet can help manage weight, promoting overall physical health and potentially improving body image and self-esteem.

6. **Cognitive Function:** Proper nutrition and exercise support cognitive function. This is especially relevant for individuals with bipolar disorder, as they may experience cognitive challenges during

certain mood states. A healthy lifestyle can contribute to improved concentration, memory, and overall cognitive performance.

7. **Social Interaction and Routine:** Exercise can provide opportunities for social interaction, whether through group activities, classes, or team sports. Social support and a sense of routine can positively impact mood and overall mental health.

8. **Enhanced Medication Response:** Good nutrition and regular exercise can enhance the effectiveness of medications prescribed for bipolar disorder. Certain lifestyle factors can influence how the body metabolizes medications, and

maintaining a healthy lifestyle can optimize treatment outcomes.

9.   **Building Resilience:** Adopting a healthy lifestyle fosters resilience, helping individuals cope with the challenges of living with bipolar disorder. The combination of proper nutrition and regular exercise contributes to an overall sense of well-being and empowerment.

Daily routines are the foundation of stability for individuals managing bipolar disorder. By prioritizing consistent sleep patterns, balanced nutrition, and regular exercise, individuals can create a supportive environment for their mental health. These lifestyle choices contribute not only to the management of bipolar disorder symptoms but also to overall well-being and resilience in the face of life's challenges. Embracing a holistic approach to daily routines empowers individuals to take an active role in their mental health, fostering a sense of control and balance in their lives.

Chapter 6

Mindfulness and Stress Reduction

Living with bipolar disorder can be a rollercoaster ride, often accompanied by periods of intense stress and emotional turbulence. Incorporating mindfulness techniques into daily life offers individuals with bipolar disorder a valuable set of tools for stress reduction, enhancing emotional regulation, and promoting overall well-being. In this chapter, we'll explore various techniques for stress management and delve into the specific benefits of mindfulness meditation for individuals navigating the complexities of bipolar disorder.

Techniques for Stress Management

Stress management is crucial for individuals with bipolar disorder, as stress can trigger episodes and exacerbate symptoms. Here are various techniques that can be effective for stress management in bipolar patients:

1. **Mindfulness Meditation:** Mindfulness meditation involves staying present in the moment without judgment. Regular mindfulness practice can help individuals manage stress by promoting relaxation and reducing anxiety. Here are some considerations for incorporating mindfulness meditation:

- **Consult with Healthcare Professionals:** Before starting any mindfulness or meditation practice, consult with your healthcare team, including psychiatrists and therapists. They can provide guidance on whether mindfulness is appropriate for you and how to integrate it safely.

- **Start Slowly:** Begin with short sessions of mindfulness meditation, gradually increasing the duration over time. Starting with just a few minutes can help prevent potential triggers or overstimulation.
- **Choose Appropriate Techniques:** Mindfulness meditation encompasses various techniques. Focusing on the breath, body scan, and loving-kindness meditation are common practices. Choose techniques that resonate with

you and are less likely to trigger mania or hypomania.

- **Regular Schedule:** Establish a consistent schedule for meditation. Routine can be beneficial for individuals with bipolar disorder, providing a sense of stability. Morning sessions may be preferable to avoid potential interference with sleep.

- **Mindful Movement Practices:** Incorporate mindful movement, such as yoga or tai chi. These practices combine physical activity with mindfulness and can be gentler for some individuals.

- **Awareness of Triggers:** During meditation, be aware of thoughts and feelings without judgment. Pay attention to any signs of triggers and adjust your practice accordingly.

- **Adapt to Mood States:** Be flexible with the practice based on your mood states. During manic or hypomanic episodes, consider shorter and more grounding practices. During depressive episodes, opt for gentle practices.

- **Combine Mindfulness with Other Strategies:** Mindfulness can be part of a broader wellness plan that includes medication, therapy, and lifestyle adjustments. It should not replace conventional treatments but complement them.

- **Mindfulness-Based Therapies:** Explore mindfulness-based therapies, such as

Mindfulness-Based Cognitive Therapy (MBCT), which is designed to prevent the recurrence of depressive episodes. These structured programs are often led by trained professionals.

- **Monitor and Adjust:** Regularly check in with your mental health professionals to discuss your meditation practice. If there are concerns or changes in mood, be open to adjusting the practice or overall treatment plan.

2. **Deep Breathing Exercises:** Deep breathing exercises, such as diaphragmatic breathing or progressive muscle relaxation, can activate the body's relaxation response, helping to alleviate stress and promote a sense of calm.

3. **Yoga:** Yoga combines physical postures, breath control, and meditation. It has been shown to reduce stress, anxiety, and improve mood. Yoga also provides a gentle form of exercise that can be adapted to different fitness levels.

4. **Progressive Muscle Relaxation (PMR):** PMR involves systematically tensing and then relaxing different muscle groups in the body. This technique can help release physical tension and promote a sense of relaxation.

5. **Cognitive-Behavioral Therapy (CBT):** CBT is a therapeutic approach that helps individuals identify and change negative thought patterns. Learning to reframe stressful thoughts can be particularly

beneficial for managing stress in individuals with bipolar disorder.

6. **Time Management:** Effective time management can help individuals with bipolar disorder reduce the stress associated with deadlines and daily responsibilities. Breaking tasks into manageable steps and prioritizing them can contribute to a sense of control.

7. **Social Support:** Maintaining a strong support system is vital for managing stress. Talking to friends, family, or support groups can provide emotional support and practical advice.

8. **Exercise:** Regular physical activity has numerous benefits, including stress reduction. Exercise releases endorphins,

which are natural mood lifters, and helps regulate sleep patterns, contributing to overall stress management.

9. **Journaling:** Keeping a journal allows individuals to express their thoughts and feelings, providing an outlet for stress. It can also help identify patterns and triggers, aiding in the development of coping strategies.

10. **Art and Music Therapy:** Engaging in creative activities like art or music can be therapeutic. These activities provide a means of self-expression and can serve as a distraction from stressors.

11. **Biofeedback:** Biofeedback involves using electronic monitoring to gain awareness and control over physiological

processes, such as heart rate or muscle tension. Learning to control these processes can aid in stress reduction.

12. **Aromatherapy:** Certain scents, such as lavender or chamomile, are believed to have calming effects. Using aromatherapy through essential oils or candles may contribute to stress reduction.

13. **Setting Boundaries:** Establishing clear boundaries in personal and professional life can help manage stress. Learning to say no when necessary and prioritizing self-care are essential aspects of boundary setting.

14. **Hobbies and Leisure Activities:** Engaging in enjoyable and relaxing

hobbies provides an opportunity for distraction and enjoyment, helping to alleviate stress.

Mindfulness and stress reduction techniques offer individuals with bipolar disorder a proactive approach to managing the challenges of their condition. By cultivating mindfulness, individuals can develop resilience in the face of stressors, improve emotional regulation, and create a foundation for stability. Incorporating these techniques into daily life empowers individuals to take an active role in their mental health, fostering a sense of control and well-being. As part of a comprehensive treatment plan, mindfulness practices contribute to a holistic approach to managing bipolar disorder and nurturing mental health.

Chapter 7

Cognitive Behavioral Strategies

Cognitive-behavioral strategies are powerful tools in the arsenal of mental health management, particularly for individuals dealing with conditions like bipolar disorder. These strategies, rooted in the principles of cognitive-behavioral therapy (CBT), focus on identifying and transforming negative thought patterns while concurrently fostering the development of healthy coping mechanisms. In this chapter, we'll explore the transformative impact of CBT in managing mental health, with a specific emphasis on reshaping thought processes and building resilient coping strategies.

Identifying and Changing Negative Thought Patterns

Cognitive Behavioral Therapy (CBT) is a widely used therapeutic approach that has shown effectiveness in helping individuals with bipolar disorder by addressing negative thought patterns and promoting healthier cognitive and behavioral responses. Here's how CBT can aid bipolar patients in identifying and changing negative thought patterns:

1. **Identification of Negative Thought Patterns:** CBT involves helping individuals become aware of their thoughts and identifying patterns that contribute to negative emotions. In the case of bipolar disorder, this might involve recognizing

thought patterns associated with depressive or manic episodes. Here are examples of negative thought patterns commonly associated with bipolar disorder:

- **Catastrophizing:**
    - *Negative Thought:* "If I don't finish this task perfectly, my whole life will fall apart."
    - *Challenge:* Explore more realistic outcomes and the possibility of handling challenges effectively even if things don't go perfectly.
- **All-or-Nothing Thinking (Black-and-White Thinking):**
    - *Negative Thought:* "If I can't do everything, I'm a complete failure."

- *Challenge:* Recognize and challenge the extreme view by acknowledging shades of gray and the possibility of making progress without perfection.

- **Overgeneralization:**

  - *Negative Thought:* "I failed at one thing, so I'm a failure in every aspect of my life."

  - *Challenge:* Identify specific instances and recognize that one setback doesn't define your entire identity or competence.

- **Mind Reading:**

  - *Negative Thought:* "Everyone at the party thinks I'm boring and doesn't want me here."

- *Challenge:* Challenge assumptions by considering alternative perspectives and recognizing that you can't accurately know what others are thinking.

- **Filtering (Selective Abstraction):**

  - *Negative Thought:* "I received positive feedback on my project, but I'm choosing to focus on the one criticism."

  - *Challenge:* Acknowledge positive aspects and avoid fixating solely on the negative.

- **Emotional Reasoning:**

  - *Negative Thought:* "I feel worthless, so I must be worthless."

- *Challenge:* Recognize that feelings are not always reflective of reality and challenge negative thoughts with evidence to the contrary.

- **Personalization:**

  - *Negative Thought:* "My friend canceled our plans; it must be because they don't like me."

  - *Challenge:* Consider alternative explanations for external events and recognize that not everything is a reflection of your worth or likability.

- **Should Statements:**

  - *Negative Thought:* "I should be able to handle this without any help."

  - *Challenge:* Replace "should" with more realistic and compassionate statements, acknowledging that it's okay to seek support when needed.

- **Labeling:**
  - *Negative Thought:* "I made a mistake; I'm such a failure."
  - *Challenge:* Reframe mistakes as opportunities for growth rather than assigning a global and negative label to oneself.

- **Discounting the Positive:**
  - *Negative Thought:* "That positive feedback doesn't count because they were just being nice."
  - *Challenge:* Acknowledge and appreciate positive feedback without minimizing or discounting it.

2. **Challenge and Restructure Negative Thoughts:** Once negative thought patterns are identified, CBT involves challenging and restructuring those thoughts. This may involve asking questions like, "Is there evidence to support this thought?" or "Are there alternative explanations?" By evaluating the accuracy of thoughts, individuals can develop a more balanced and realistic perspective.

3. **Monitoring Mood Swings:** CBT often includes mood monitoring, where individuals track their mood fluctuations, identifying triggers, and associated thought patterns. This can help patients become more aware of the connections

between their thoughts, emotions, and behaviors.

4. **Behavioral Activation:** CBT includes behavioral strategies to complement cognitive work. Behavioral activation involves encouraging individuals to engage in activities that bring a sense of accomplishment and pleasure, even during low or high mood states. This can disrupt negative thought patterns by changing the context and reinforcing positive behaviors.

5. **Problem-Solving Skills:** CBT equips individuals with bipolar disorder with problem-solving skills to address challenges and stressors. This can prevent the escalation of negative

thoughts and emotions and empower individuals to take constructive actions.

6. **Developing Coping Strategies:** CBT helps individuals develop effective coping strategies to manage stress and mood swings. This may include relaxation techniques, mindfulness exercises, and other skills that can be used to counteract negative thought patterns.

7. **Setting Realistic Goals:** Setting and achieving realistic goals is an essential aspect of CBT. This helps individuals build a sense of accomplishment, counteracting feelings of hopelessness that can accompany negative thought patterns during depressive episodes.

8. **Relapse Prevention:** CBT provides tools for recognizing early warning signs of mood swings and developing strategies to prevent relapse. By identifying and addressing negative thought patterns, individuals are better equipped to manage their condition over the long term.

Cognitive-behavioral strategies provide a structured and evidence-based approach to managing mental health, particularly in the context of bipolar disorder. By identifying and transforming negative thought patterns, individuals can break the cycle of destructive thinking and reduce the impact on their mood. Simultaneously, the development of healthy coping mechanisms equips individuals with practical tools to navigate life's challenges. When integrated into a comprehensive treatment plan, cognitive-behavioral strategies empower individuals to take an active role in their mental health, fostering resilience, and enhancing overall well-being.

Chapter 8

Journaling for Emotional Regulation

Journaling, a simple yet powerful tool, has proven to be an effective means of promoting emotional regulation and mental well-being. For individuals navigating the challenges of emotional volatility, such as those with bipolar disorder, journaling serves as a cathartic outlet and a method for gaining insight into mood patterns and triggers. Let's explore the therapeutic power of writing, particularly in the context of emotional regulation, and delve into the benefits of tracking moods and triggers through journaling.

The Therapeutic Power of Writing

"The therapeutic power of writing" refers to the practice of expressive writing as a means of promoting emotional well-being and mental health. This approach can be particularly beneficial for individuals with bipolar disorder, providing a creative outlet for self-reflection, mood management, and personal growth. Here are several ways in which writing can be therapeutic for a bipolar patient:

1. **Self-Expression:** Writing allows individuals with bipolar disorder to express their thoughts, emotions, and experiences in a safe and private space. This can be especially valuable during periods of intense emotions, providing an

outlet for self-expression and catharsis.

2. **Mood Tracking:** Keeping a mood journal can help individuals track their emotional states over time. This can be useful for recognizing patterns, identifying triggers, and gaining insights into the relationship between mood and daily life events. For someone with bipolar disorder, mood tracking through writing can be a valuable tool for self-awareness and managing mood swings.

3. **Coping Strategy Development:** Writing can serve as a platform to explore and develop coping strategies. Individuals can document what has worked well for them in the past and brainstorm new techniques for managing stress, anxiety,

or depressive symptoms. This reflective process can contribute to a personalized toolbox of coping mechanisms.

4. **Goal Setting and Planning:** Writing allows individuals to set and articulate personal goals. Breaking down larger goals into smaller, manageable steps and documenting progress can provide a sense of accomplishment and motivation. This process aligns with cognitive-behavioral principles and can be particularly helpful for individuals with bipolar disorder.

5. **Narrative Therapy:** Writing can be a form of narrative therapy, helping individuals construct and reframe their life stories. This can be empowering, allowing

individuals to reinterpret past experiences and envision a positive and hopeful future.

6. **Enhancing Self-Awareness:** Regular writing encourages self-reflection and greater self-awareness. This heightened awareness can help individuals identify early signs of mood changes, allowing for proactive interventions and better self-management of bipolar symptoms.

7. **Creative Exploration:** Engaging in creative writing, such as poetry or fiction, provides an avenue for imaginative expression. Creative exploration can be a powerful way to channel intense emotions, offering an alternative means of processing and communicating

feelings.

8. **Stress Reduction:** The act of writing can be a meditative and calming practice. Taking the time to put thoughts on paper can be a form of mindfulness, promoting relaxation and reducing stress. This can be particularly beneficial during manic or anxious phases.

9. **Building Resilience:** Writing about challenging experiences, setbacks, and personal triumphs can contribute to the development of resilience. Chronicling one's journey with bipolar disorder and reflecting on moments of resilience can serve as a source of inspiration during difficult times.

10. **Communication with Therapists:** Written reflections can be shared with mental health professionals during therapy sessions, providing valuable insights into the individual's experiences, thought patterns, and progress. This enhances the therapeutic alliance and facilitates more targeted interventions.

Journaling stands as a powerful and accessible tool for individuals seeking emotional regulation, offering a multifaceted approach to mental well-being. As an integral part of a holistic self-care routine, journaling empowers individuals with tools for self-reflection, emotional understanding, and proactive coping. In the journey toward emotional regulation, the humble journal becomes a steadfast companion, fostering resilience and promoting mental health.

Chapter 9

Relationships and Communication

Building and maintaining healthy relationships is a cornerstone of emotional well-being, and for individuals navigating the complexities of bipolar disorder, effective communication becomes even more critical. Let's explore the principles of nurturing healthy relationships and delve into strategies for communicating effectively about bipolar disorder to foster understanding and connection.

Nurturing Healthy Relationships

Maintaining healthy relationships can be challenging for individuals with bipolar disorder, as the condition is characterized by extreme mood swings that can affect one's thoughts, emotions, and behaviors. However, with the right strategies and support, individuals with bipolar disorder can nurture and sustain healthy relationships. Here are some tips for individuals with bipolar disorder to foster positive connections:

1. **Open Communication:** Honest and open communication is crucial. Individuals with bipolar disorder should communicate their needs, triggers, and boundaries to their partners, friends, and family. Encourage your loved ones to express their feelings as well, fostering a safe and understanding environment.

2. **Education:** Educate yourself and your loved ones about bipolar disorder. Understanding the condition can help demystify the mood swings and behaviors associated with it. Share information about your treatment plan and how your loved ones can support you during different phases of the disorder.

3. **Medication and Treatment Compliance:** Consistently follow your treatment plan, which may include medication, therapy, and lifestyle adjustments. This can help stabilize mood swings and contribute to more predictable behavior. Keep your loved ones informed about your treatment plan and involve them in discussions with mental health

professionals when appropriate.

4. **Establish Routine:** Establishing a daily routine can provide stability and predictability. Regular sleep, exercise, and meals contribute to better mood regulation. Share your routine with your loved ones so they can understand and support your efforts to maintain stability.

5. **Recognize Triggers:** Be aware of your triggers for mood episodes and communicate them to your loved ones. This helps both you and your partners/family members anticipate and navigate potential challenges. Work together to develop coping strategies for managing triggers when they arise.

6. **Seek Support:** Encourage your loved ones to seek their own support networks. This might involve therapy, support groups, or education on how to best support someone with bipolar disorder. Consider involving your partner or family members in therapy sessions to facilitate understanding and communication.

7. **Self-Care:** Prioritize self-care to maintain emotional and physical well-being. This includes getting enough rest, engaging in activities you enjoy, and managing stress. Communicate your self-care needs to your loved ones, and encourage them to engage in their own self-care practices.

8. **Crisis Plan:** Develop a crisis plan with your mental health professionals and loved

ones. This plan can outline steps to take during a mood episode, including who to contact and what actions to take.

9. **Flexibility and Patience:** Recognize that both you and your loved ones will need to be flexible and patient. Mood episodes can be challenging, but a supportive and understanding environment can make a significant difference.

10. **Celebrate Successes:** Acknowledge and celebrate your successes, no matter how small. This can contribute to a positive atmosphere and reinforce the importance of ongoing efforts.

Communicating Effectively about Bipolar Disorder

Communicating effectively about bipolar disorder is essential for building understanding, fostering support, and maintaining healthy relationships. Here are some tips on how to communicate effectively about bipolar disorder:

1. **Educate Yourself:** Before discussing bipolar disorder with others, make sure you have a good understanding of the condition. Knowledge about symptoms, treatment options, and potential challenges can help you communicate more confidently and accurately.

2. **Choose the Right Time and Setting:** Find an appropriate time and setting to

talk. Choose a quiet, comfortable place where you can have privacy and ample time for the conversation without interruptions.

3.   **Use Clear and Simple Language:** When discussing bipolar disorder, use clear and straightforward language. Avoid jargon or technical terms unless you're sure the person you're talking to understands them. This helps to avoid confusion and ensures a more accessible conversation.

4.   **Share Personal Experiences:** Share your own experiences with bipolar disorder, explaining how it affects your thoughts, emotions, and behaviors. Personalizing the conversation can make it more relatable and help others

empathize with your situation.

5. **Express Emotions:** Share your emotions and feelings about living with bipolar disorder. This can help others understand the impact it has on your life and the challenges you may face. Be honest and open about both positive and negative aspects.

6. **Discuss Treatment and Coping Strategies:** Explain your treatment plan and the strategies you use to manage bipolar symptoms. This might include medication, therapy, lifestyle adjustments, and self-care practices. Emphasize the importance of consistency in treatment.

7. **Highlight Triggers and Warning Signs:** Discuss specific triggers or warning signs of mood episodes. This information can help others recognize when you might need additional support and understand the context of certain behaviors.

8. **Encourage Questions:** Invite questions and be prepared to answer them. Encouraging others to ask questions shows that you are open to dialogue and helps dispel any misconceptions or concerns they may have.

9. **Provide Resources:** Offer educational resources about bipolar disorder. This could include pamphlets, books, or reputable websites that provide more information. This allows others to

educate themselves further and promotes a shared understanding.

10. **Set Boundaries:** Clearly communicate any boundaries or specific needs you may have. This helps others understand how they can support you effectively and respect your limits.

11. **Acknowledge Challenges and Celebrate Successes:** Be honest about the challenges you face, but also highlight the successes and progress you've made. This balanced approach can provide a more comprehensive picture of your journey with bipolar disorder.

12. **Involve Mental Health Professionals:** If appropriate, involve mental health professionals in the conversation. This

could include inviting a therapist or psychiatrist to join a discussion with family members to provide additional insights and guidance.

13. **Revisit the Conversation:** Recognize that understanding may not happen immediately. Revisit the conversation as needed, providing updates on your condition, treatment progress, and any changes in your needs or preferences.

Navigating relationships while managing bipolar disorder requires a delicate balance of communication, understanding, and support. Nurturing healthy relationships involves open communication, emotional support, and mutual respect. When addressing bipolar disorder, effective communication strategies such as choosing the right time, using "I" statements, and encouraging active listening can enhance understanding and foster a supportive environment. By working together, individuals and their partners can build strong, resilient relationships that contribute positively to mental well-being and overall quality of life.

Chapter 10

Workplace Strategies

For individuals with bipolar disorder, achieving success in the workplace involves a delicate balance of managing responsibilities while navigating the complexities of their mental health condition. Let's now explore effective workplace strategies, focusing on how individuals with bipolar disorder can balance their work responsibilities and make informed decisions about disclosing their condition in the professional sphere.

Balancing Work Responsibilities

Managing work responsibilities while coping with bipolar disorder can be challenging, but with the right strategies and support, individuals with bipolar disorder can lead fulfilling professional lives. Here are some tips on how a bipolar patient can effectively balance work responsibilities:

1. **Understand Your Triggers:** Identify and understand your personal triggers for mood swings and episodes. This awareness can help you anticipate and manage potential challenges in the workplace.

2. **Medication Adherence:** Consistently take prescribed medications as directed by your healthcare provider. Proper

medication can help stabilize mood and reduce the risk of manic or depressive episodes.

3. **Establish a Routine:** Create a structured daily routine that includes regular sleep patterns, healthy meals, and exercise. Consistency in your routine can contribute to mood stability.

4. **Communication:** Openly communicate with your supervisor and colleagues about your condition. Discussing your needs and potential challenges can foster understanding and support in the workplace.

5. **Set Realistic Goals:** Break down your workload into manageable tasks and set realistic goals. Avoid overcommitting

yourself, and prioritize tasks based on deadlines and importance.

6. **Flexible Work Arrangements:** Explore flexible work arrangements such as flextime, telecommuting, or part-time schedules. Having some flexibility in your work environment can help you manage stress and maintain stability.

7. **Take Breaks:** Allow yourself short breaks throughout the day to recharge. Taking a few minutes to step away from your desk or workspace can help prevent burnout and improve focus.

8. **Self-Care:** Prioritize self-care activities, including regular exercise, proper nutrition, and sufficient sleep. These lifestyle factors play a crucial role in

managing bipolar disorder.

9.   **Recognize Warning Signs:** Be vigilant about recognizing early signs of mood changes. If you notice any signs of a potential episode, take proactive steps, such as adjusting your schedule or seeking support from your mental health professional.

10. **Build a Support System:** Surround yourself with a supportive network, both personally and professionally. Having friends, family, and colleagues who understand and support you can make a significant difference in managing your condition at work.

11. **Work-Life Balance:** Strive for a healthy work-life balance. Avoid overworking and

prioritize activities outside of work that bring you joy and relaxation.

12. **Employee Assistance Programs (EAPs):** Many companies offer EAPs that provide confidential counseling and support services. Take advantage of these resources if available.

Disclosing Bipolar Disorder at the Workplace

Disclosing bipolar disorder at the workplace is a personal decision, and individuals should carefully consider their own circumstances before making such a choice. Here are some considerations and tips for disclosing bipolar disorder at the workplace:

1. **Know Your Rights:** Understand your legal rights regarding disclosure. In many

countries, there are laws protecting individuals with disabilities, including mental health conditions, from discrimination in the workplace. Familiarize yourself with these laws to ensure you know your rights.

2. **Assess the Work Environment:** Evaluate the workplace culture and attitudes toward mental health. If the environment is supportive and open, you may feel more comfortable disclosing your bipolar disorder.

3. **Choose the Right Time and Place:** Select an appropriate time and place to disclose your condition. It's often best to do this in a private setting, such as during a one-on-one meeting with your supervisor or

HR representative.

4. **Prepare What You Want to Say:** Plan ahead and prepare what you want to communicate about your bipolar disorder. Be clear about how it might impact your work and what accommodations or support you might need.

5. **Focus on Abilities and Accommodations:** Emphasize your abilities and strengths. Discuss any accommodations you may need to perform your job effectively. This can help alleviate concerns and demonstrate your commitment to your work.

6. **Provide Information:** Offer basic information about bipolar disorder,

explaining what it is and how it affects you. This can help dispel misconceptions and create a more informed and understanding environment.

7. **Highlight Your Commitment to Treatment:** If applicable, mention your commitment to treatment, such as regular therapy or medication. This can reassure your employer that you are actively managing your condition.

8. **Request Confidentiality:** Clearly state that you would like the information to remain confidential. While employers have a responsibility to provide reasonable accommodations, they are generally not allowed to share your medical information without your

consent.

9. **Be Open to Questions:** Be open to questions or concerns your employer or colleagues may have. This can foster understanding and may help dispel any myths or misconceptions about bipolar disorder.

10. **Seek Support:** If you're unsure about disclosing, seek advice from a mental health professional, a support group, or a trusted colleague who has experience with mental health disclosure.

11. **Monitor Changes in Treatment:** If your treatment plan changes and it might impact your work, consider discussing these changes with your supervisor or HR to ensure that appropriate

accommodations are in place.

12. **Build a Support Network:** Cultivate a support network within the workplace. Having allies and advocates can make the disclosure process more manageable and provide ongoing support.

Successfully navigating the workplace with bipolar disorder involves a combination of effective strategies for balancing responsibilities and making informed decisions about disclosure. Establishing a structured routine, setting realistic goals, and maintaining open communication contribute to a positive work experience. When it comes to disclosure, understanding one's rights, assessing the workplace culture, and focusing on necessary accommodations empower individuals to make choices that support both their mental health and professional success. By integrating these strategies, individuals with bipolar disorder can thrive in the workplace while maintaining stability and well-being.

Chapter 11

Creativity and Self-Expression

Creativity and self-expression stand as powerful tools for individuals navigating the complexities of bipolar disorder. Engaging in artistic pursuits not only provides an outlet for emotions but also serves as a therapeutic means of navigating the highs and lows of mood swings. In this chapter, we'll explore the transformative potential of creativity, focusing on exploring art, writing, and other outlets, as well as the profound impact of channeling emotions through creative expression.

Exploring Art, Writing, and Other Outlets

Exploring art, writing, and other creative outlets can be therapeutic and beneficial for individuals with bipolar disorder. Engaging in creative activities provides a way to express emotions, manage stress, and promote overall well-being. Here are some ways in which art, writing, and other outlets can be helpful for someone with bipolar disorder:

1. **Art Therapy:**

- **Benefits:** Art therapy can help individuals express and explore emotions that may be challenging to verbalize. It provides a nonverbal means of communication and can be a valuable tool for self-discovery.

- **Activities:** Painting, drawing, sculpture, and other visual arts can be incorporated into art therapy. Creating art can serve as a form of meditation and relaxation.

2.   **Writing as Expression:**

- **Benefits:** Writing allows individuals to articulate their thoughts and feelings, providing a structured outlet for self-reflection. Journaling, poetry, and creative writing can be particularly therapeutic.

- **Activities:** Keeping a mood journal, writing poetry, or creating a personal narrative can help process experiences and track emotional patterns.

3.   **Music and Movement:**

- **Benefits:** Music has a powerful impact on mood and emotions. Engaging in music or dance activities can provide an outlet for self-expression and a way to release pent-up energy.

- **Activities:** Playing an instrument, listening to music, or participating in dance can be enjoyable and contribute to emotional regulation.

4.   **Photography and Visual Arts:**

- **Benefits:** Capturing images or creating visual art can provide a different perspective on the world. It encourages mindfulness and attention to the present moment.

- **Activities:** Photography, collage, and mixed media art allow for creative expression through visual elements.

5. **Creative Writing Workshops:**

- **Benefits:** Participating in creative writing workshops or groups can foster a sense of community and provide a structured environment for sharing experiences.

- **Activities:** Joining a writing group, whether in-person or online, can offer support, feedback, and a sense of connection with others who share similar experiences.

6. **Mindfulness Meditation through Art:**

- **Benefits:** Combining mindfulness practices with art can enhance self-awareness and focus. It can be particularly useful for managing stress and anxiety.

- **Activities:** Mindful coloring, mandala creation, or other meditative art practices can be incorporated into a mindfulness routine.

7. **Collaborative Projects:**

- **Benefits:** Engaging in collaborative art or writing projects can foster social connections and a sense of purpose. Working on projects with others can provide mutual support and encouragement.

- **Activities:** Participating in community art projects, group writing exercises, or collaborative art installations can be both rewarding and socially enriching.

8. **Artistic Exploration as a Coping Mechanism:**

- **Benefits:** Engaging in creative activities can serve as a healthy coping mechanism during different mood states. It provides an alternative focus and can be a source of joy and accomplishment.

- **Activities:** Encouraging exploration of different artistic mediums allows individuals to discover what resonates best with them.

Creativity and self-expression offer individuals with bipolar disorder a transformative and empowering means of navigating their emotional landscape. By exploring art, writing, and various creative outlets, individuals can channel their emotions, foster self-discovery, and build resilience. Creative expression becomes a valuable companion on the journey to managing bipolar disorder, providing solace, insight, and a tangible way to connect with oneself and others. Embracing the therapeutic power of creativity opens doors to self-discovery, personal growth, and a renewed sense of purpose.

Chapter 12

Facing Relapses

Living with bipolar disorder involves navigating a journey marked by highs and lows, and setbacks are an inevitable part of this complex landscape. Recognizing warning signs of relapse and developing effective coping strategies are essential components of managing setbacks. In this chapter, we'll explore the importance of recognizing warning signs and provide strategies for individuals with bipolar disorder to bounce back from difficult times.

Recognizing Warning Signs of Relapse

Recognizing signs of relapse in bipolar disorder is important for individuals and their support networks to intervene early and manage the condition effectively. Here are signs of a potential relapse in bipolar disorder:

1. **Changes in Mood:**

   - **Mania:** Elevated mood, increased energy, racing thoughts, impulsivity, heightened irritability, decreased need for sleep, and engaging in risky behaviors.

   - **Depression:** Persistent sadness, low energy, fatigue, feelings of worthlessness or guilt, changes in sleep patterns (insomnia or hypersomnia), changes in appetite, difficulty concentrating, and thoughts of death or suicide.

2. **Sleep Disturbances:** Significant changes in sleep patterns, such as insomnia or hypersomnia, can be indicators of an impending relapse. For example, decreased need for sleep during a manic episode or increased need for sleep during a depressive episode.

3. **Irritability:** Unexplained irritability, impatience, or anger that is disproportionate to the situation may signal a shift in mood.

4. **Changes in Activity Level:** Sudden changes in activity levels, such as

increased restlessness, impulsivity, or hyperactivity during a manic episode, or a noticeable decrease in energy and motivation during a depressive episode.

5. **Impaired Judgment:** Poor decision-making, engaging in risky behaviors, or acting impulsively without regard for consequences can be indicative of a manic episode.

6. **Social Withdrawal:** A decrease in social interactions or withdrawal from activities that were previously enjoyed may be a sign of depression.

7. **Cognitive Changes:** Difficulty concentrating, racing thoughts, or impaired judgment can occur during manic episodes. Conversely, cognitive

slowing, indecisiveness, and difficulty focusing may be signs of depression.

8. **Changes in Self-Care:** Neglecting personal hygiene, changes in grooming habits, or a lack of interest in self-care can be indicative of a depressive episode.

9. **Changes in Speech:** Rapid or pressured speech during mania, or slowed and lethargic speech during depression, can be observed.

10. **Physical Symptoms:** Changes in appetite, weight gain or loss, and other physical symptoms like headaches or stomachaches may accompany mood changes.

11. **Increased Substance Use:** A sudden increase in alcohol or substance use may

be a coping mechanism or a symptom of a manic or depressive episode.

12. **Difficulty in Relationships:** Strained relationships with family, friends, or colleagues may occur due to mood fluctuations, irritability, or social withdrawal.

Strategies for Bouncing Back from Difficult Times

Experiencing a relapse in bipolar disorder can be challenging, but with effective strategies, individuals can work towards recovery and stability. Here are some strategies for bouncing back from a bipolar relapse:

1. **Reach Out for Professional Help:** Contact your mental health professional

immediately to discuss your symptoms and develop a plan for managing the relapse. Adjustments to medications or therapy may be necessary.

2. **Reestablish Routine:** Reestablish a daily routine that includes regular sleep patterns, healthy meals, and consistent exercise. A structured routine can contribute to stability and help regulate mood.

3. **Set Realistic Goals:** Break down tasks into manageable goals. Setting realistic and achievable objectives can help rebuild confidence and a sense of accomplishment.

4. **Gradual Return to Responsibilities:** Ease back into work and other responsibilities

gradually. Overloading yourself immediately after a relapse can be overwhelming. Start with small tasks and gradually increase your workload.

5. **Seek Social Support:** Reach out to friends, family, or support groups. Sharing your experiences with those who understand can provide emotional support and reduce feelings of isolation.

6. **Therapeutic Support:** Increase the frequency of therapy sessions or consider additional therapeutic support. Cognitive-behavioral therapy (CBT) or other evidence-based approaches can help you manage stress and develop coping strategies.

7. **Medication Adherence:** Ensure strict adherence to your medication regimen. If changes in medication were made during the relapse, follow up with your healthcare provider to discuss their effectiveness and potential adjustments.

8. **Self-Monitoring:** Keep a mood journal to track your emotions, energy levels, and any triggers that may contribute to mood fluctuations. This can help you and your healthcare provider identify patterns and make informed decisions about your treatment plan.

9. **Healthy Lifestyle Choices:** Prioritize self-care, including regular exercise, balanced nutrition, and sufficient sleep. These lifestyle factors play a crucial role in

overall mental health.

10. **Mindfulness and Relaxation Techniques:** Practice mindfulness, meditation, or relaxation techniques to manage stress and promote a sense of calm. These techniques can be valuable in preventing future relapses.

11. **Educate Yourself and Loved Ones:** Learn more about bipolar disorder and educate your loved ones. Increased understanding can lead to better support and communication within your social network.

12. **Crisis Plan:** Develop a crisis plan with your mental health professional. This plan should outline specific steps to take in the event of worsening symptoms or a

potential relapse. Share this plan with trusted individuals in your support network.

13. **Engage in Activities You Enjoy:** Reconnect with activities that bring you joy and relaxation. Engaging in hobbies and interests can contribute to a positive mood and a sense of purpose.

14. **Celebrate Small Achievements:** Acknowledge and celebrate small achievements. Recognize and appreciate the progress you make, no matter how minor. Positive reinforcement can be motivating.

15. **Reflect and Learn:** Reflect on the factors that may have contributed to the relapse and discuss them with your

healthcare provider. Learning from these experiences can help you develop better coping strategies for the future.

Coping with setbacks in bipolar disorder is a multifaceted journey that requires self-awareness, support, and proactive strategies. Recognizing warning signs of relapse empowers individuals to intervene early, while developing effective coping strategies helps them bounce back from difficult times. Through a combination of self-care, support networks, and ongoing collaboration with healthcare professionals, individuals with bipolar disorder can navigate setbacks with resilience and emerge stronger on their mental health journey.

Chapter 13

Looking Toward the Future: Setting Goals and Dreams

Living with bipolar disorder does not preclude the pursuit of meaningful goals and dreams. In fact, setting and working towards personal and professional aspirations can be a crucial component of long-term stability. In this chapter, we'll explore the importance of planning for stability and the strategies for pursuing personal and professional goals while managing bipolar disorder.

Planning for Long-Term Stability

Planning for long-term stability with bipolar disorder involves a comprehensive and proactive approach to managing the condition. Here are strategies to help individuals with bipolar disorder achieve and maintain long-term stability:

1. **Build a Support System:** Cultivate a strong support network that includes family, friends, and mental health professionals. Having a reliable support system can provide emotional support and assistance during challenging times.

2. **Regular Mental Health Monitoring:** Stay vigilant about monitoring your mental health. Keep a mood journal to track your emotions, energy levels, and any triggers

or patterns that may indicate changes in mood.

3. **Adherence to Treatment Plan:** Consistently adhere to your treatment plan, which may include medication, therapy, and lifestyle changes. Regularly check in with your healthcare provider to discuss the effectiveness of your current treatment and make any necessary adjustments.

4. **Therapy and Counseling:** Engage in regular therapy, such as cognitive-behavioral therapy (CBT) or dialectical behavior therapy (DBT). Therapy can provide coping strategies, stress management techniques, and tools for handling challenging situations.

5. **Medication Management:** Work closely with your psychiatrist to find the right medication and dosage. Be open about any side effects or concerns you may have. Regularly review and adjust your medication plan as needed.

6. **Healthy Lifestyle Choices:** Prioritize a healthy lifestyle, including regular exercise, balanced nutrition, and sufficient sleep. These factors can positively impact mood and overall well-being.

7. **Establishing a Routine:** Create and maintain a consistent daily routine. A structured routine can help regulate sleep patterns, reduce stress, and contribute to stability.

8. **Identify and Manage Triggers:** Identify potential triggers for mood episodes and develop strategies to manage or avoid them. This may involve stress reduction techniques, lifestyle adjustments, and communication with your support network.

9. **Crisis and Wellness Plan:** Develop a crisis and wellness plan in collaboration with your mental health professional. This plan should outline specific steps to take in the event of a crisis or worsening symptoms, as well as strategies for maintaining wellness.

10. **Education and Advocacy:** Educate yourself and your loved ones about bipolar disorder. Understanding the

condition can empower you to make informed decisions and advocate for your needs in both personal and professional settings.

11. **Regular Medical Checkups:** Schedule regular checkups with your healthcare providers, including routine physical exams. Monitoring your overall health is essential, as physical health can impact mental well-being.

12. **Employment and Career Planning:** Discuss your condition with your employer if necessary, and explore workplace accommodations that can support your well-being. Consider a career that aligns with your strengths and allows for a reasonable work-life balance.

13. **Financial Planning:** Develop a financial plan to manage potential challenges related to employment, treatment costs, and other financial stressors. This may involve budgeting, saving, and exploring financial assistance programs.

14. **Continued Learning and Skill Development:** Continuously invest in personal and professional development. Acquiring new skills and knowledge can enhance your confidence and resilience.

15. **Mindfulness and Stress Reduction:** Practice mindfulness, meditation, or other stress reduction techniques. These practices can promote emotional regulation and resilience in the face of life's challenges.

Pursuing Personal and Professional Aspirations

Pursuing personal and professional aspirations while managing bipolar disorder requires a thoughtful and proactive approach. Here are some strategies to help individuals with bipolar disorder navigate their personal and professional lives effectively:

Personal Strategies

1. **Self-Awareness:** Develop a deep understanding of your own triggers, warning signs, and patterns of mood fluctuations. Self-awareness is key to managing bipolar disorder effectively.

2. **Consistent Self-Care:** Prioritize self-care activities, including regular exercise,

adequate sleep, and a balanced diet. Establishing and maintaining healthy habits contributes to overall well-being.

3. **Therapy and Support Groups:** Engage in therapy to learn coping strategies, stress management techniques, and ways to navigate challenges. Support groups can provide a sense of community and understanding.

4. **Mindfulness and Stress Reduction:** Practice mindfulness, meditation, or other stress reduction techniques to enhance emotional regulation and resilience.

5. **Open Communication:** Communicate openly with trusted friends, family, and colleagues about your condition. Sharing

your experiences can foster understanding and support.

6. **Set Realistic Goals:** Establish achievable short-term and long-term goals. Break larger goals into smaller, manageable tasks to build a sense of accomplishment.

7. **Flexibility:** Be flexible and adaptable in your approach to personal aspirations. Understand that there may be times when adjustments are necessary, and that's okay.

8. **Monitor Mood and Seek Help:** Regularly monitor your mood and seek professional help if you notice signs of a potential relapse or worsening symptoms.

9. **Establish Boundaries:** Set boundaries to protect your mental health. Learn to

say no when needed and communicate your limits to others.

10. **Celebrate Successes:** Acknowledge and celebrate your achievements, no matter how small. Positive reinforcement can boost motivation and confidence.

Professional Strategies

1. **Disclosure and Workplace Accommodations:** Consider disclosing your condition to your employer if you believe it will benefit you. Discuss workplace accommodations that may support your well-being without compromising your professional goals.

2. **Career Planning:** Choose a career that aligns with your strengths and interests. Consider factors such as work

environment, flexibility, and job satisfaction when making career decisions.

3. **Work-Life Balance:** Prioritize work-life balance to prevent burnout. Set realistic expectations and boundaries to maintain stability.

4. **Flexible Work Arrangements:** Explore flexible work arrangements, such as part-time schedules or telecommuting, if feasible. Discuss these options with your employer to create a work environment that supports your needs.

5. **Time Management:** Develop effective time management skills to enhance productivity. Break tasks into smaller, manageable steps and prioritize based on

deadlines and importance.

6. **Build a Supportive Network:** Cultivate a supportive professional network. Surround yourself with colleagues who understand and respect your condition.

7. **Continuous Learning:** Invest in continuous learning and skill development. Stay updated in your field to remain competitive and pursue professional growth.

8. **Financial Planning:** Develop a financial plan to manage potential challenges related to employment and treatment costs. Budgeting and saving can provide a sense of financial security.

9. **Emergency and Crisis Plan:** Establish a plan for handling emergencies or crisis

situations at work. Communicate this plan with trusted colleagues or supervisors.

10. **Advocate for Yourself:** Advocate for your needs in the workplace. If necessary, seek guidance from human resources to ensure your rights are protected.

Setting and pursuing goals with bipolar disorder requires a holistic approach that prioritizes stability, self-awareness, and resilience. Planning for long-term stability involves consistent medication management, therapeutic engagement, a strong support network, and lifestyle adjustments. Pursuing personal and professional aspirations entails goal setting, career planning, continuous education, balancing ambition with well-being, networking, and embracing creativity. By combining effective mental health management with strategic goal setting, individuals with bipolar disorder can look toward the future with optimism, knowing that they have the tools and support needed to achieve their dreams.

Conclusion

In the tapestry of life, each thread contributes to the rich and complex narrative of our existence. As we reach the conclusion of "Coping with Bipolar: Practical Tools for Daily Living," it is with a profound acknowledgment that the journey through bipolar disorder is not linear but rather a mosaic of experiences, challenges, and triumphs. This book has aimed to be a companion, a guide, and a source of strength for those grappling with the intricate dance of highs and lows.

The practical tools shared within these pages are not meant to be a panacea but rather lanterns that cast light on the path toward understanding, self-compassion, and resilience. Coping with bipolar disorder is not a destination; it is an ongoing process of self-discovery and adaptation. We conclude this exploration with the recognition that each individual's journey is unique, and there is no one-size-fits-all solution. However, in the diversity of experiences and strategies, there lies a tapestry of collective wisdom that binds us together.

As we part ways, may the lessons learned here echo in the hearts and minds of readers, offering solace during the stormy days and a compass during the sunlit ones. Let this book be a reminder that within the ebb and flow of bipolar disorder, there is strength, resilience, and the potential for a fulfilling life. To every reader seeking understanding and support, may you find comfort in the knowledge that you are not alone.

This is not the end but a continuation of a journey—a journey toward a life marked by acceptance, empowerment, and the unwavering belief that, even in the face of bipolar disorder, there is a path to not only cope but to thrive.